THE MAYFLOWER AND THANKSGIVING HISTORY
Pilgrims Edition
2nd Grade U.S. History Vol I

SPEEDY
PUBLISHING

The Mayflower voyage has become an iconic story in some of the earliest annals of American history, with its story of death and of survival in the harsh New England winter environment.

The Mayflower was the name of the sailing ship that took the people, who would become known collectively as the 'Pilgrims', to the New World.

The Mayflower was
a three-masted ship,
most likely between
90 and 110 feet long.

There were 102 passengers and between 25-30 crew members.

The owner of the
Mayflower was
Christopher Jones
who was also the
captain of the ship.

The Mayflower and the
Speedwell originally left
Southampton, England
on August 4, 1620.

At Plymouth they decided to leave the Speedwell behind because it was leaking and crowded as many passengers as they could on the Mayflower. They left Plymouth on September 6, 1620.

Traveling as a passenger on the Mayflower was very difficult.

There were no
bathrooms on the
Mayflower and the
passengers had
to wear the same
clothes every day
for 66 days.

Over two months after
leaving Plymouth,
the Mayflower
reached Cape Cod on
November 9, 1620.

They sent out scouting parties in smaller boats to find a place to live and discovered an area which had forests and fresh-water streams. This was where they created the Plymouth Colony.

Harbor Cruises
Next cruise departs at
HARBOR CRUISES

Thanksgiving Day is
a national holiday
celebrated in Canada
and the United States.

It is celebrated as a
day of giving thanks
for the blessing of
the harvest and of
the preceding year.

In the United States Thanksgiving is observed on the fourth Thursday in November.

In Canada it occurs
on the second
Monday of October.

By the fall of 1621 only half of the pilgrims, who had sailed on the Mayflower, survived. The survivors, thankful to be alive, decided to give a thanksgiving feast.

The tradition of Thanksgiving started with the Pilgrims who settled at Plymouth, Massachusetts. They first held a celebration of their harvest in 1621. The feast was organized by Governor William Bradford.

The first time they called the feast "Thanksgiving" was in 1623, after rain had ended a long drought.

The first national
Thanksgiving Day
was proclaimed by
President George
Washington in 1789.

Visit
BABY PROFESSOR
EDUCATION KIDS
www.BabyProfessorBooks.com
to download Free Baby Professor eBooks
and view our catalog of new and exciting
Children's Books